Daniel Radcliffe

ABDO
Publishing Company

Big Buddy BOOKS
Buddy Bios

by **Sarah Tieck**

VISIT US AT
www.abdopublishing.com

Published by ABDO Publishing Company, 8000 West 78th Street, Edina, Minnesota 55439.

Printed in the United States of America, North Mankato, Minnesota.
112009
012010

 PRINTED ON RECYCLED PAPER

Coordinating Series Editor: Rochelle Baltzer
Contributing Editors: Heidi M.D. Elston, Megan M. Gunderson, BreAnn Rumsch, Marcia Zappa
Graphic Design: Maria Hosley
Cover Photograph: *AP Photo*: Brian Zak/Sipa/Press/Sipa via AP Images
Interior Photographs/Illustrations: *AP Photo*: Tammie Arroyo (p. 12), Dave Caulkin (p. 13), Jason DeCrow (p. 5),
    Shizuo Kambayashi (p. 28), Press Association via AP Images (p. 16), Paul Sancya (p. 24), Matt Sayles (p. 22),
    Sang Tan (p. 27), Ian West/PA (p. 17); *FilmMagic*: FilmMagic.com (p. 7); *Getty Images*: AFP/AFP (p. 25),
    Dave M. Benett (p. 21), Bruce Glikas (p. 21), Kayt Jones/Time & Life Pictures (p. 18), Peter Mountain (p. 15),
    Rischgitz (p. 10); *Shutterstock*: Francois Loubser (p. 8).

Library of Congress Cataloging-in-Publication Data

Tieck, Sarah, 1976-
  Daniel Radcliffe : Harry Potter star / Sarah Tieck.
    p. cm. -- (Big buddy biographies)
  ISBN 978-1-60453-973-8
  1. Radcliffe, Daniel, 1989---Juvenile literature. 2. Actors--Great Britain--Biography--Juvenile literature. I. Title.
  PN2598.R27T54 2010
  791.4302'8092--dc22
  [B]
                            2009036433

Daniel Radcliffe

Contents

Rising Star

Daniel Radcliffe is a talented actor. He has appeared in movies and plays. He is best known for acting in the Harry Potter movies. Daniel stars as the lead character, Harry Potter.

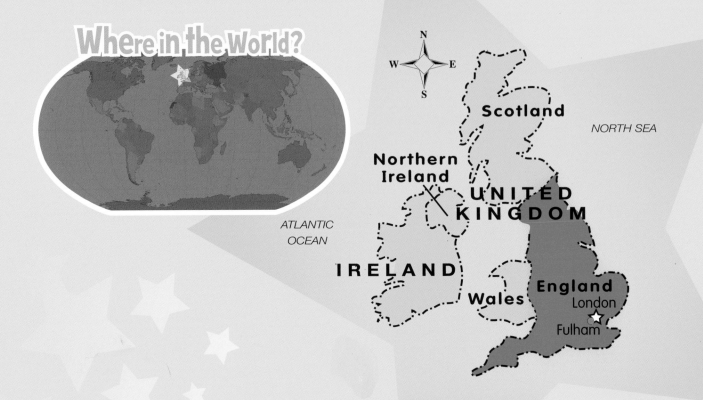

Family Ties

Daniel Jacob Radcliffe was born in Fulham, England, on July 23, 1989. Daniel is the son of Alan Radcliffe and Marcia Gresham. He has no brothers or sisters.

Daniel's mom (*above*) and dad support his work. But, they usually stay out of the spotlight.

Growing Up

Daniel grew up in Fulham. His mother worked as a casting agent. Her job was to find actors for various **roles**. Daniel's father was a literary agent. He helped authors sell their work.

Did you know...

Daniel loves music. He listens to his favorite bands. And he can play bass guitar!

Daniel attended Sussex House School and then City of London School. He was a good student. Daniel learned about theater and music in some of his classes.

London is a large city located on the river Thames. Many smaller cities, such as Fulham, make up the Greater London area.

Did you know...

David Copperfield is by British author Charles Dickens. The story was first printed in many parts. Then in 1850, this famous work became a book.

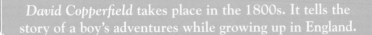
David Copperfield takes place in the 1800s. It tells the story of a boy's adventures while growing up in England.

A Young Actor

Daniel knew he wanted to be an actor at age five. His parents weren't sure if he should become an actor. But, people kept encouraging him.

Finally, Daniel's parents let him **audition** for a television movie called *David Copperfield*. In 1999, Daniel got his first lead **role** as young David Copperfield. This was an important role. It helped people notice Daniel's talent.

Jamie Lee Curtis is a famous American actress. She acted in her first movie in 1977.

In 2001, Daniel appeared in *The Tailor of Panama*. For this movie, he worked with actress Jamie Lee Curtis. Around this time, casting agents were looking for actors for the first Harry Potter movie. Many young actors were **auditioning** to play Harry Potter. Jamie Lee told Daniel's mother that Daniel looked like the boy **wizard**.

13

Did you know...

The Tailor of Panama is an adventure story. It is based on a book by John le Carré.

Daniel had just a small part in *The Tailor of Panama*. Still, it helped him feel more sure of himself when playing Harry Potter.

Becoming Harry

At first, Daniel's parents didn't want their son to try out for Harry Potter. They were afraid Daniel would be let down. Then, they ran into the movie's **producer** at a play. He convinced them to let Daniel **audition** for the **role**.

Daniel was 11 years old when he got the role of Harry Potter. He was very excited! Soon, he started filming *Harry Potter and the Sorcerer's Stone*. This is the first movie in the Harry Potter **series**.

Daniel says becoming Harry is one of the most exciting things that has ever happened to him.

Did you know...

The Harry Potter books and movies are about a boy named Harry. Harry learns he is a wizard and attends wizard school. There, he has many adventures and battles evil.

15

Lights! Camera! Action!

The Harry Potter movies are based on J.K. Rowling's popular book **series**. Eight movies were made from seven books. The first movie was **released** in 2001. Daniel played the **role** of Harry in all eight movies.

During filming, Daniel became close friends with Rupert Grint and Emma Watson. Their acting skills improved as they worked on each movie. Daniel also became friends with older Harry Potter actors, such as Kenneth Branagh.

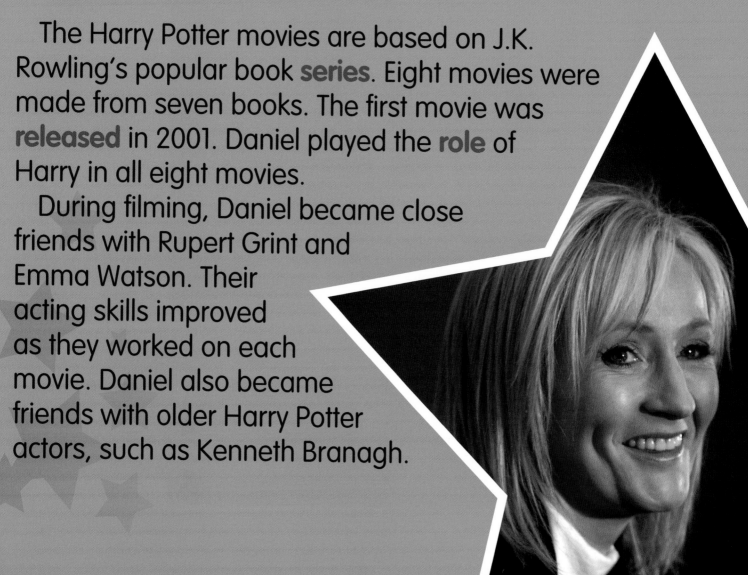

In the Harry Potter movies, Harry's close friends are Hermione and Ron. Emma (*center*) plays Hermione, and Rupert (*right*) plays Ron.

While working on the Harry Potter movies, Daniel got to know J.K. Rowling.

LIFE

AMERICA'S WEEKEND MAGAZINE

HOLIDAY MOVIE MAGIC

10 DON'T-MISS FAMILY FILMS

Rupert, Emma, and Daniel became so popular that their pictures were on magazine covers.

Welcome Back, POTTER

Rupert Grint, Emma Watson, and Daniel Radcliffe (from left) of *Harry Potter and the Goblet of Fire*

Did you know...

Daniel did some of his own stunts in the Harry Potter movies. Stunts are actions that require great skill or daring.

The Harry Potter movies were very successful. People liked Daniel's acting in the movies, and he gained many fans. People came to think of him as Harry Potter.

Daniel became a movie star! Reporters often **interviewed** him. And, he appeared in magazines and newspapers.

On the Stage

In addition to movies, Daniel has acted in plays. In 2007, he performed in the play *Equus* in London. He had the lead **role**. Many people saw Daniel as more grown up after this.

In 2008, Daniel performed *Equus* in New York City, New York. He acted on Broadway. Broadway shows are considered some of the best in the country.

Performing live is different from performing for a camera. Daniel learned new acting skills from the director and cast of *Equus*.

Daniel won two Broadway.com Audience Awards for his work in *Equus*. Audience members choose the winners of these awards.

BROADWAY.COM
2009
Favorite Le...   ...e Broadway Play

Did you know...

Daniel can memorize most lines if he reads them three times. He says it took him six times to memorize his Harry Potter lines.

Fans and reporters often take Daniel's picture.

An Actor's Life

Daniel may work several hours each day when making a movie. He practices lines and sometimes learns special skills for his **roles**. Then, he gets into **costume** and shoots scenes. Daniel also travels all over the world. He attends movie openings and meets fans.

Since the Harry Potter books and movies are so popular, toys and games have been created.

The Harry Potter movies broke sales records all over the world. Their success has helped Daniel gain more acting opportunities. Some of his other movies include *My Boy Jack* and *December Boys*.

Fans often wait in long lines to see Harry Potter movies.

Off the Screen

When Daniel is not working, he spends time with his family and friends. He likes to play funny tricks on them. Daniel also enjoys writing. He's written poems about characters he imagined.

Daniel helps others. He gives his time and money to charities. He asks fans to give money to charities he likes.

As Rupert, Emma, and Daniel
completed the Harry Potter movies,
they began to work on separate projects.

Daniel enjoys meeting fans. Sometimes he signs autographs for them.

Buzz

Daniel's fame continues to grow. In 2009, he filmed scenes for *Harry Potter and the Deathly Hallows*. This is the last book in the Harry Potter **series**. It will be **released** as two movies in 2010 and 2011.

Daniel plans to keep acting. Fans are excited to see what's next for Daniel Radcliffe.

Snapshot

★**Name**: Daniel Jacob Radcliffe

★**Birthday**: July 23, 1989

★**Birthplace**: Fulham, England

★**Appearances**: *David Copperfield, The Tailor of Panama, the Harry Potter movies, December Boys, Equus, My Boy Jack*

Important Words

audition (aw-DIH-shuhn) to give a trial performance showcasing personal talent as a musician, a singer, a dancer, or an actor.

charity a group or a fund that helps people in need.

costume clothing worn to help show a certain time period, person, place, or thing.

interview to ask someone a series of questions.

producer a person who oversees the making of a movie, a play, an album, or a radio or television show.

release to make available to the public.

role a part an actor plays.

series a set of similar things or events in order.

wizard a person who is skilled in magic.

Web Sites

To learn more about Daniel Radcliffe, visit ABDO Publishing Company online. Web sites about Daniel Radcliffe are featured on our Book Links page. These links are routinely monitored and updated to provide the most current information available.

www.abdopublishing.com

Index